by Dean Raymond

SCHOOL PUBLISHERS

Cover ©Photodisc; 3 ©Robert I.M. Campbell/National Geographic Image Collection;
4 ©Photodisc; 5 ©Harcourt Education Australia/Lewis Chandler; 6 ©Robert I.M. Campbell/National
Geographic Image Collection; 7 ©Harcourt Education Australia/Lewis Chandler;
8 ©Robert I.M. Campbell/National Geographic Image Collection; 9 ©Peter G. Veit/National
Geographic Image Collection; 10–11 ©Robert I.M. Campbell/National Geographic Image Collection;
12–13 ©Alamy/Steve Bloom Images; 14 ©APL/Corbis.

Printed in China

ISBN 10: 0-15-350443-9
ISBN 13: 978-0-15-350443-3

Ordering Options
ISBN 10: 0-15-350332-7 (Grade 2 Below-Level Collection)
ISBN 13: 978-0-15-350332-0 (Grade 2 Below-Level Collection)
ISBN 10: 0-15-357452-6 (package of 5)
ISBN 13: 978-0-15-357452-8 (package of 5)

4 5 6 7 8 9 10   0940   15 14 13 12 11 10 09

Dian Fossey is remembered for her work with gorillas. In 1963, she went to Central Africa. There she saw mountain gorillas for the first time. These wonderful animals became a part of her life.

Gorillas are rare animals. Dian was surprised by how big they were. She noticed how their large, black bodies blended into the thick forest.

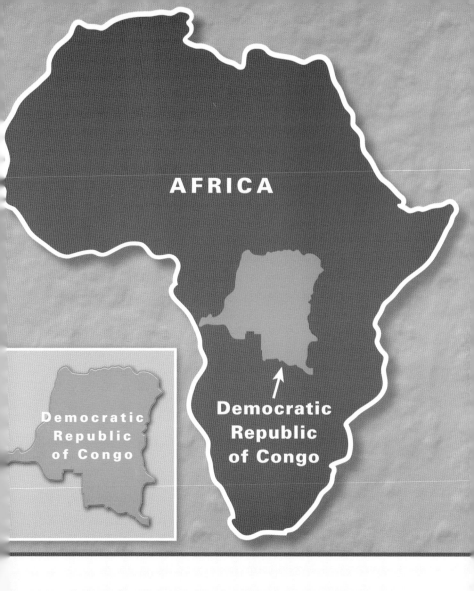

AFRICA

Democratic
Republic
of Congo

Democratic
Republic
of Congo

Dian studied mountain gorillas
in the Congo in 1966. At first, she
watched them quietly from a distance.

Later, Dian made gorilla noises.
She hoped the gorillas would get used
to her. After six months, they let her
come closer.

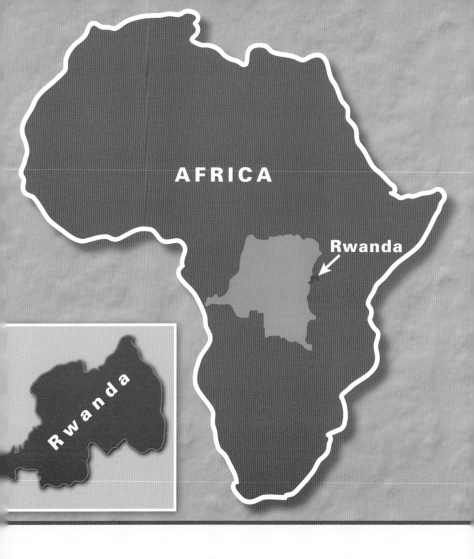

Then in 1967, Dian moved from the Congo to Rwanda. There she studied a new group of mountain gorillas. They were not used to people.

Dian wanted to show the gorillas
that she did not want to harm them.
She did this by going up to them on her
hands and knees.

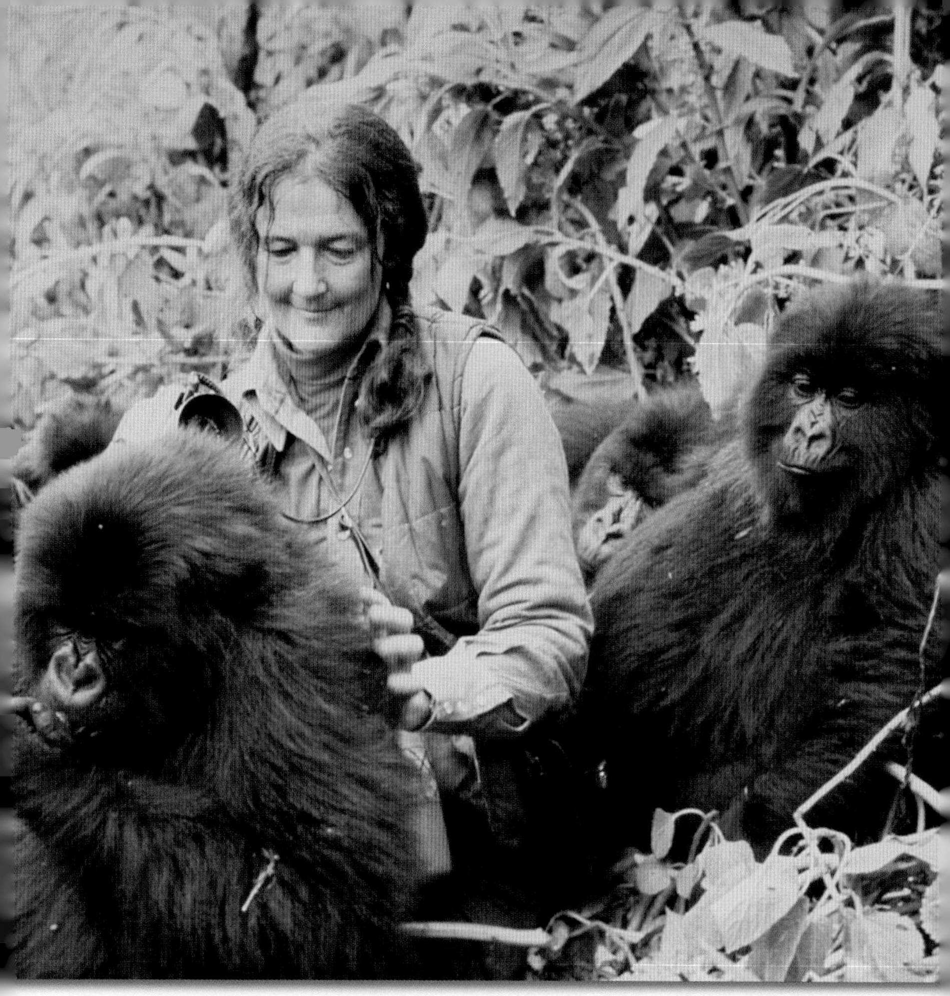

At last, she could sit with them. She noticed that the gorillas had different personalities. She gave them names. Some even reminded her of people she knew!

One day, she was sitting with the gorillas. A young gorilla she called Peanuts came over and touched her. She had made a friend!

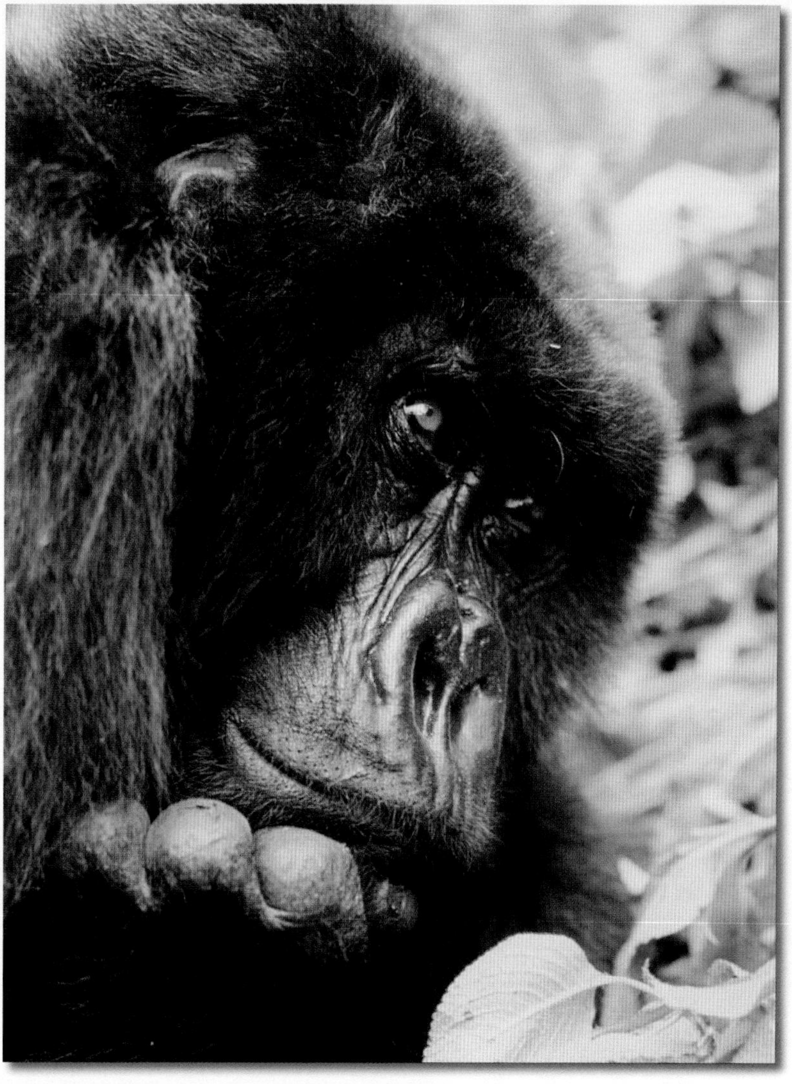

Dian's favorite gorilla was called Digit. He would play with her hair or softly tap her with crumpled leaves.

One day in 1976, Dian was watching the gorillas. They were sitting together. Suddenly, a wet, raggedy gorilla cradled her with its arm.

It was Digit! Digit looked at Dian and patted her head. They sat together in the rain.

Dian wrote down what she learned about mountain gorillas. Today, many people go to Africa to see the gorillas in the wild.

Think Critically

1. What places did Dian Fossey visit to study the gorillas in 1966 and 1967?

2. What were some of the things Dian did to earn the trust and friendship of the gorillas?

3. What are two things you can tell about Rwanda from the map on page 7?

4. What words could be used to describe Dian Fossey?

5. What do you think about people trying to get very close to wild animals?

Science

Gorilla Facts Draw a gorilla on a large sheet of paper or cardboard and then cut it out. Inside the gorilla shape, list some of the facts you learned from the book.

 School-Home Connection Tell someone at home about Dian Fossey's adventures. Ask that person why they think Dian wanted to find out so much about the gorillas.